The Secrets in Your Name

Discovering the Real You.

by Sandra McKenzie

0 43422 69574 4

Written by Sandra McKenzie
Cover Design by Design Dynamics, Glen Ellyn, Il
Typography by Dmitry Feygin

Published by Great Quotations Publishing Co.,
Glendale Heights, IL

ISBN 1-56245-304-1

Library of Congress Catalog Card Number: 97-071656

Printed in Hong Kong

Dedicated to
my mother:

Wyneta Farr McKenzie Messick

and to friends:

William Staley and Jody Rowe Staley

and to my
Native American Indian grandmother:

Laura South McKenzie Terhune

Preface

People came from miles around and lined up outside my grandmother's house for her to foretell their future reading tarot cards and, unknown to them, the energies in their birth names and nicknames.

For years I fought against using the talent she passed on to me. However, while working for major corporations and striving for success in sales, I found myself inadvertently practicing by intuition what she overtly did for years.

Eventually I discovered that reading the energies in names was perhaps a little known ancient art or science which is just now starting to surface.

Using this art, I've come to realize that reading energies in the first and middle letters of names is a quick way of knowing the basics about people whether for love, friendship, work, etc. Try it!

Ambitious, Clever, Loyal

The **A** Personality:

"A" must be the ring leader. You're self-made. You've concocted the picture that you want the world to see, and no one's going to get beneath it without your permission.

Even though life dealt you hardships before you were a teen, you adapted, if uneasily. Perhaps this background created your ambitious nature.

A's need to be first in everything—in ideas and action. You might pooh-pooh the good ideas of others, then secretly implement them. While you strive to possess the best, you won't show off what you have, but you must appear as if you're a person of means.

You can tend to be well-known in your field, or you land in jail trying to make a name for yourself. When you lose your temper, it happens so quickly that others don't see it coming. They're astonished, saying, "What did I do?" That's because you hide anger with charisma for a short period of time; but

8

when you lose it, you go all the way.

Spiritually, you take nothing for granted. Personally, you are very independent, and you insist on doing things for yourself – in your own stubborn way. **A**'s are very loyal.

The **A** *Colors:*

Gold   Red
Navy Blue   White

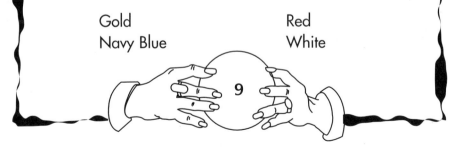

9

The **A** Love Compatibility Guide:

You live to be the clever one getting the best of everyone—the more famous, the better. You may have a lot of people surrounding you, but you prefer only a handful of friends. You stand alone spiritually and personally.

Sure Thing: J L P Q R U Z
Possibilities: E F G V W
Avoid: A B C D H I K M N O S T X Y

10

Suggested Occupations for the Typical **A**:

In order to get what an **A** wants, you work on several projects at the same time, hoping that something will come through in a big way. Usually it does. When working with people, **A**'s prefer relating only with males.

Accountant
Apartment Manager
Attorney
Camera Operator

Collection Agent
Director
Gangster
Producer

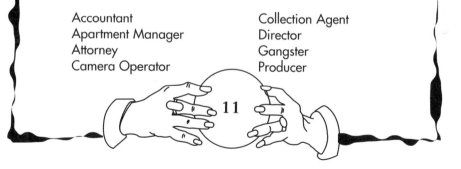

11

Extremist, Obstinate, Spiritual

The **B** Personality:

B's fight two sides. You want to be independent, but at the same time you want to be close.

As a child it's possible that you were loved, then mistreated, or maybe both. It broke your trusting nature. It also affected your ability to forgive, and you're likely to be obstinate in whatever you're asked to do.

When a gift needs to be given to you, one big expensive

gift is better than a lot of little ones. But maybe a check is better because you must have money.

B has to get plenty of fruits, vegetables and water into your diet because your digestive system is sensitive to your emotions. You have an impossible time letting go of anything – money, jobs and relationships. You name it. So a balanced diet is a must.

You're an extremist. You can be messy or clean, wordy or

silent, with ups and downs. If you are offended, a **B** will try harder than anyone to prove that the other person was wrong.

You fight yourself. You want to be with someone, but you don't want to be tied down. Make up your mind. While **B**'s are spiritual, it's difficult for you to accept that God is everywhere.

The **B** *Colors:*

Emerald   all Pastels
Green in all shades   Pink
Light Blue

The **B** Love Compatibility Guide:

B loves grandeur and must share riches quietly with that one very unique person. A mate is important. You won't spend your life alone. You cherish the past, and if you forget a family event, you're remorseful.

<u>Sure Thing:</u>	D G H I M N S Y
<u>Possibilities:</u>	B L O P U
<u>Avoid:</u>	A C E F J K Q R T V W X Z

Suggested Occupations for the Typical **B***:*

You must work where everyone is being treated with the same importance, and you function well in a team as long as you're told, "You're doing a good job." Those words are emotionally necessary for your self-esteem.

Animal Caretaker
Bank Teller
Choreographer

Cosmetologist
Veterinarian

Creative, Curious, Charming

The **C** Personality:

"C" is definitely a Mary Poppins who springs back after bad news. You look at the world through rose-colored glasses and have to be hit on the head for a dose of reality.

You must always understand a circumstance entirely. No unsolved puzzles for **C**'s. You should always be studying something because you learn quickly, especially if you can touch what you're learning. You get bored easily, which

19

drove your parents crazy when you were a child!

C's become curious about something and start it; then something more curious comes up and you'll start that, too, because nothing holds your attention. You don't always finish what you start. You investigate things thoroughly before starting them, then vow to finish what you began. You enjoy being in a group because you love hearing everyone's opinion.

20

And when you nod your head "yes," it only means that a person's entitled to his own opinion.

When people think they have a meeting of the minds with you, they're surprised to see that suddenly a **C** is off on a ninety degree angle from the agreed-upon path. Your curiosity won again. You must learn to stay the course after you've arrived at a decision.

C's could have two of everything: two pairs of tennis shoes exactly alike, two lovers or a shirt of the same style in different colors. You will listen to all ideas for spiritual improvement.

The **C** *Colors:*

Beige   Purple
Navy Blue   Yellow

22

The **C** *Love Compatibility Guide:*

C's relate to all ages because you appeal to the youthful qualities which are present in everyone. You're nervous, impatient and compulsive, so you don't always think things through.

<u>Sure Things:</u>   F J L P Q U
<u>Possibilities:</u>   D H N R V W X
<u>Avoid:</u>   A B C E G I K M O S T Y Z

23

Suggested Occupations for the Typical **C**:

You're creative, sharing, social, charming and have a very inquisitive mind.

Chef
Child Care Worker
Computer Analyst
Controller

Customer Sevice Representative
Elementary Teacher
Nurse

24

Loyal, Creative, Handy

The **D** Personality:

"D" can do fifty things at the same time, so don't get involved with someone who is lazy. You couldn't cope. And when tasks pile up, you get to the bottom.

When you were a child, there was some family conflict. You did something important for them, but the family never thanked you. Now as an adult, you must be appreciated. If you don't hear the words, "We know you give up a lot for us," a **D** can leave home and create a family of friends. However, you can't totally abandon family and responsibilities, for you are loyal and have a hard time cutting the cord. You might not like it, but you will help if family calls.

A **D** has a deep-seated anger about something not said or something not done which needs to be resolved with positive action. You can write down your hostilities on a piece of paper and go into the backyard, burn the paper, say prayers over the ashes, then cover the ashes with soil and forget the past. Consider writing a letter to those toward which you have a hostility and thank them for at least one thing each one may have given you, even if only for genes you inherited, and then watch the hostility disappear.

You need to discuss the pros and cons of any major decision you're considering with someone who will listen. Once you get it all out, you'll go make your own decision.

D can collect anything. You will get out your sword to defend friends and family, and you expect the same in return. Get fruits, vegetables and water into your diet.

The **D** Colors:

Alabaster	Gray
Cream	Turquoise
Beige	Violet
Blue	

28

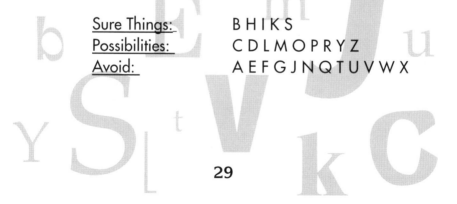

The **D** Love Compatibility Guide:

You're creative and love rituals and family.

Sure Things: B H I K S
Possibilities: C D L M O P R Y Z
Avoid: A E F G J N Q T U V W X

29

Suggested Occupations for the Typical **D***:*

You're excellent in using your hands and great at repetitive work.

Assembly Worker
Costume Designer
Day Care Center

General Contractor
Real Estate Broker
Restaurateur

Logical, Outspoken, Spiritual

The **E** Personality:

"E" has a variety of jobs. The upside is that, if you've educated yourself, you can do many different things. The down side is that you can do so many different things, you have a hard time focusing on the one thing that you really can do best. What complicates your choice of occupations is that you can be physically and mentally active. Whatever job you pursue, you must work around people where you can solve problems and, at the same time, be totally in control of yourself. So you don't scatter your energies, you might take an occupational choice test at a local college to help define and keep you on the right career path.

You will stay with something or someone for a long time but then suddenly make some change in a major area of your life: give up a position, move to a new home or form a partnership. Your ups and downs are partially because you don't edit what comes out of your mouth. At times you can be misinterpreted. People have strong opinions about you, and it's never neutral. You love knowledge and money, but knowledge probably wins.

33

You can be spiritual, but you sometimes fight boredom and sometimes look for excitement in the wrong directions.

The **E** *Colors:*

Beige	Purple
Navy Blue	Yellow

The **E** Love Compatibility Guide:

E has a strange way of loving. You become bigger than life and the person you love becomes smaller. You believe your mate thinks the same way you do. You must remember that other people have their own thoughts, desires and opinions. If a person becomes like you, you'll become bored and leave.

<u>Sure Things:</u>   F J L P U V W
<u>Possibilities:</u>   A H R
<u>Avoid:</u>   B C D E G I K M N O Q S T X Y Z

Suggested Occupations for the Typical **E***:*

You can be a public speaker, a writer or maybe even a travel agent or a therapist, since you approach problems with logic.

Artist
Athlete
Commentator
Mechanic

Newspaper Writer
Therapist
Travel Agent

36

Ambitious, Leader, Religious

The **F** Personality:

"F" almost pulls off living two lives. No one can be more responsible than you when you're responsible, for you can own your own company or run someone else's. But the other side of you can go on spurts of escapades which can happen at the oddest times.   It's hard for people to understand your changeability. Your two sides fight each other. The trouble-some side becomes imaginative in adventures and takes risks.

You did not get to live out all of your childhood because of some parental conflict. As an adult, you suddenly might break away from your responsibilities, throw them to the wind and perform adult behaviors in a childlike way. You might jeopardize the life you've built for romantic encounters, substance abuse or perhaps some money-making scheme or risky speculation.

An **F** badly needs praise, but if it's not forthcoming, you will do something to get it. You can go to extremes. You can be an excellent social worker because you love listening to people's problems.

While you shine at a party you can suddenly become introverted and expect other people to come to you and recognize your worth. If they don't, an **F** gets hurt feelings because you're sensitive about what others might be thinking.

You can be religious and obsessive about sharing the information with everyone close to you.

The **F** Colors:

Emerald Green	Royal Blue
Gold	Wine
Orange	Yellow
Red	

The **F** Love Compatibility Guide:

You love family, and an **F** must be in love – preferably with a partner who loves to keep balance and oneness. Your partner must plan surprises to keep you from taking diversions with others.

<u>Sure Things:</u>	C E J L P X
<u>Possibilities:</u>	A U Z
<u>Avoid:</u>	B D F G H I K M N O Q R S T V W Y

Suggested Occupations for the Typical **F**:

You're ambitious and an excellent leader if you learn not to control or manipulate and instead lead by example.

Administrator
Engineer
Fire Fighter
Mathematician

Postmaster
Social Worker
Waiter/Waitress

Realistic, Responsible, Efficient

The **G** Personality:

"G", when asked, "Do you love me?" might answer, "I washed your car for you, didn't I?" You demonstrate your love to people, but your partner needs to hear those magical words, "I'm mad about you, darling!" That's hard for you to say because you rely only upon yourself, which makes you appear to be withdrawn.

44

You may take a long time before you make a decision because you weigh the pros and cons. But when it's important, you can make a quick decision.

You like realistic and dependable situations. You also want to know ahead of time what you're going to be doing for the day. Then you settle down to the job and complete it systematically, even enhancing what other people have developed.

45

While routine is up your alley, you require time alone to think it through and get it done efficiently. You try everything possible to avoid arguments.

You will help the miserable, the misinterpreted or those who are having problems adapting. One of the beautiful things about you is that you embrace people just the way they are without trying to change them into something you would rather they be.

46

You also don't like forcing your views upon others. However, you need to project some of your own thoughts to other people. It will help your self-worth. Whatever goal a **G** sets, it will be done to perfection. You accept your own financial responsibility.

The **G** *Colors:*

Brown   Navy Blue
Green   Sapphire Blue

The **G** Love Compatibility Guide:

When it comes to love, stop keeping your feelings to yourself. You're too reserved.

<u>Sure Things:</u>   B H I S T Y Z
<u>Possibilities:</u>   A G J L N P Q U
<u>Avoid:</u>   C D E F K M O R V W X

Suggested Occupations for the Typical **G**:

A **G** makes a great social worker because people can come to you and be heard. You can also be a school administrator or run a company.

Chemist
Electrician
Herbalist
Kineseologist

Librarian
Property Manager
Scientist
Truck Driver

Capable, Creative, Secretive

The **H** Personality:

An **"H"** must be in the business world. However, at home, the family might suffer because you spend too much time trying to make it big at work.

You need to balance being a good family member at home along with your work load at the office, so that each gets equal time and dedication.

You jump hoops for anyone who pays attention to you. If no one shows appreciation, you might orchestrate events to get it.

But if an **H** gets acknowledgment in the right way by doing the right things, then the other energies of money and fortune also come. While **H**'s are creative, you can be secretive if it's something that others would not approve of.

The beginning of your life seems to be full of responsibility. It isn't until around midlife that you look at the world around you, ready to play, and wonder where the family is. Don't be surprised if they don't need you emotionally after you've neglected them in favor of providing material possessions for all those years. They're not ungrateful; they just don't know you. If the family is still available, you may have to mend fences.

When you hit a big windfall, put seventy percent of it aside. Only reinvest the other thirty percent so that the money picture doesn't go to extremes.

Balance in everything is the key word in your life, in emotions and money. If you understand balance, most everything else can come to you in the right way quite abundantly.

The **H** colors:

Brown	Pumpkin
Forest Green	Yellow

The **H** Love Compatibility Guide:

You feel that destiny plays an important part in your life. Maybe it does, but don't put all of your faith in it. Take control yourself.

<u>Sure Things:</u>   B D G I M N O V
<u>Possibilities:</u>   C E H L P S T X
<u>Avoid:</u>   A G J K Q R U W Y Z

Suggested Occupations for the Typical **H**:

H is very capable of being in a top executive position where everyone respects you.

Antique Dealer
Casino Dealer
Financial Manager
General Manager

Mechanic
Physical Therapist
Special Education Teacher

Emotional, Creative, Inflexible

The **I** Personality:

"I" must have money in the bank in order to feel that all the bases are covered. It doesn't have to be a big balance, but enough to feel safe.

You'll go out of your way to help people because you want them to need you. You might read a tragic story in the newspaper about a local person who needs money, and you could easily rush out to help him with a contribution of money or clothing because you really feel for his plight.

57

Watch your stomach because life and its stresses play havoc on your emotions and your stomach pays the price. I's are highly emotional, and your life can be full of regular ups and downs.

Though you like to keep life on an even keel, you have a really hard time not getting your feelings hurt when people don't see things exactly the way you do. You feel secure when family members are close to you. You don't like an empty nest, and you work very hard to keep balance and peace in the family. You love having them rely on you.

58

It would not be unusual for you to associate yourself with famous people, for everyone seems to love you. Watch that you don't have a tendency to also feel famous.

You like surroundings of beauty. You're creative, plodding, methodical and inflexible. You could have several occupations at the same time.

The **I** *Colors:*

Emerald	all Pastels
Green in all shades	Pink
Light Blue	

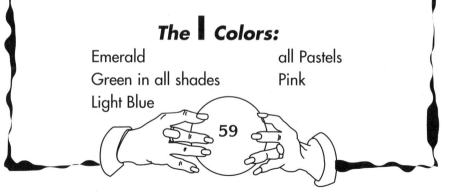

The I Love Compatibility Guide:

You're definitely in love with love more than anyone else.
That's because you don't really know who you are. In your
mind love seems to give you definition in your relationships
with other people.

Sure Things: B G H I R S
Possibilities: D M N O Y
Avoid: A C E F J K L P Q T U V W X Z

60

Suggested Occupations for the Typical **I**:

An **I** is talented in many areas, mainly creative.

Architect
Art Collector
Beautician
Cabinet Maker

Counselor
Landscape Artist
Restaurant Hostess

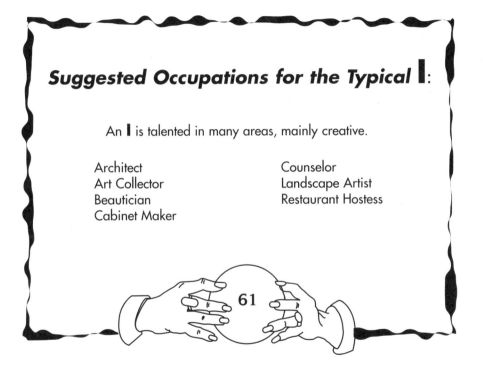

61

Assertive, Independent, a Leader

The **J** Personality:

"J" loves learning, and if you've prepared yourself through education, you can be a leader. You have a hard time arriving at a decision because you're busy weighing the pros and cons.

You can be both physically and mentally agile at the same time. **J** may dream, but you fulfill your goals without being prodded. You're assertive. And since you really depend upon only yourself, you are your own best partner. That's why it's hard for you to keep a mate.

Gratitude is not a big word in your vocabulary. **J**'s have a hard time even saying, "Thank you" until you're older. It's not deliberate.

You just don't see when friends and relatives go out of their way for you. You wear blinders. You may not be generous enough to those who are closest to you, yet you could be a humanitarian and give your money away to strangers.

J must learn that what's good for the goose is good for the gander. You can tell someone off for doing something that you might turn around and do, then justify having done it.

Truth doesn't hit you over the head until you're in your early thirties. You might try to run from your problems. Don't. Solve them so you don't have to face them again.

You go through a lot of changes in your life, but you perform admirably during a real crisis.

The J Colors:

All shades of Blue   Turquoise
Purple

The J Love Compatibility Guide:

You don't negotiate. You do things your own way. You can even put love on the back burner while you're busy with your obligations.

<u>Sure Things:</u>	A C E F L P Q X
<u>Possibilities:</u>	G J N R U V
<u>Avoid:</u>	B D H I K M O S T W Y Z

Suggested Occupations for the Typical **J**:

Nobody can stop you when you commit yourself to a task. You go for it and stay the course. But a **J** does suffer from getting bored if there aren't enough challenges.

Administrator
Broker
Executive Secretary
Factory Supervisor
Maintenance Engineer

Manager
Minister
Reporter
Teacher

Opinionated, Compulsive, Trustworthy

The **K** Personality:

"K" must feel that the family lends moral support in everything that you do. If the family does not, you can write them off and not see them for many years.

You feel very strongly about everything. That's why you can be opinionated. Nothing can deter you from your aspirations. You're a pit bull and will hang on unless you decide to change to something else.

69

You need to temper what you say and how you say it. Be gentle.
You'll find that your bowels will thank you. You can be generous or
greedy, and your friends are never quite sure what your mode or
mood is. But one thing is sure – you are a trustworthy friend. You
do not betray confidences.

You have to watch that you don't overdo anything because you
can be compulsive. Try moderation in everything. Tell people up

front not to pry into your personal business, your closet, your desk drawers, because you don't tolerate snoops. Trust your intuitive voice. It can save you grief. You always bounce back.

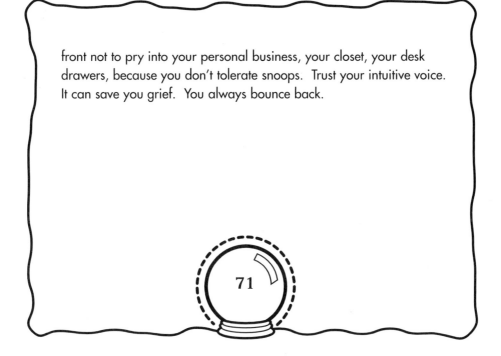

71

The **K** Colors:

Beige
Black
Bright Red
Navy

Purple
Ruby Red
Wine
Yellow

The **K** Love Compatibility Guide:

K's have quite a temper which, when you explode, can leave a meek person devastated. After you blow, like the great whale in the ocean, it's all over for you. You're on your way to bigger fish. Don't be surprised, however, if your mate is still smarting from insults when you come home.

Sure Things: D M O T Z
Possibilities: K L P S Y
Avoid: A B C E F G H I J N Q R U V W X

73

Suggested Occupations for the Typical **K**:

Don't be surprised if you don't begin your career until your early thirties. You might be busy trying several things before you settle. You're very good at getting down into the details of an occupation, so you could try spying legally, of course, by being a detective. You'd also be an excellent writer or therapist.

Actuary
Billing
Construction
Court Reporter
Detective

Photographer
Psychologist
Researcher
Stone Mason
Writer

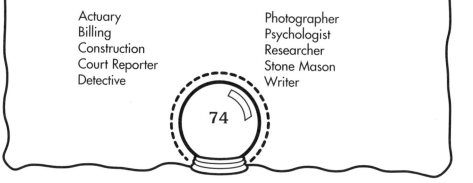

74

Generous, Social, Smart

The **L** Personality:

"L" can be a prize in all relationships if you don't become overprotective. You are a marvelous friend. You will give and continue to give in all relationships, but sometimes people take you for granted and selfishly forget to reciprocate. That can drive you into a shell, or you rebel, and suddenly people are shocked – wondering what has happened.

You need to be given back what you so generously give. **L**'s talent is loving people, serving people and bringing peace to everyone. If the world had more of you, there would be fewer wars.

When you're thinking about something, you say, "I'm going to make a decision tomorrow about X, Y or Z." That's a hint that people should tell you how they feel, and you'll consider it. You do that because you don't like hurting people's feelings. Once you arrive at a decision, it is definite.

Until then, you will listen to what other people close to you have to say. **L** is social and will comfort people with problems.

L's must have time alone to recover your energies. You tend to be nervous because your emotions get quite taxed. Subconsciously you don't make a decision until you think things through.

You're smart and funny. You could throw a party for one, yourself, and enjoy it. You're spiritual.

The **L** Colors:

Light Green   Royal Blue
Pink   White

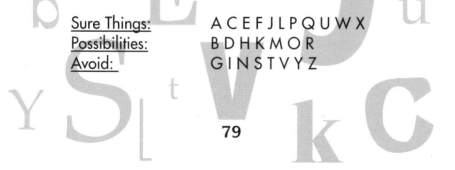

The L Love Compatibility Guide:

Sometimes you have problems in love relationships if your partner doesn't give you the full appreciation you deserve.

Sure Things: A C E F J L P Q U W X
Possibilities: B D H K M O R
Avoid: G I N S T V Y Z

Suggested Occupations for the Typical **L**:

You need to surround yourself with beauty. You could work for an art gallery, be a hairdresser in an exquisite salon, a writer, a negotiator or be employed in any position that involves helping people who need you.

Archivist	Paralegal
Art Dealer	Poet
Artist	Potter
Auctioneer	Teacher
Curator	Telephone Operator
Jeweler	Trucker

Nurturer, Organized, Loyal

The **M** Personality:

"M" is the nurturer to the troubled world. Everyone approaches you as family, and you take on their problems. Don't, unless you like being depressed. All problems are not your responsibility.

You will rescue any stray or waif, two-legged or four-legged, but some creatures are not always worthy of your help. They ask too much. But you always say, "Well, maybe this one last time will be the time that really helps."

82

After two times you should stop enabling lost causes to call on you for advice or material possessions, for others can interfere with your own partnership, experience and achievement.   And after helping others for so long, you may need a therapist yourself.   Even you must have someone who will sit down with you, not interrupt or bottom line you, and let you talk yourself out.   You must hear yourself say what you're emotionally feeling.   Then you've solved the problem.

M is constantly busy, friendly and organized.   You accept the unavoidable.   You love to vacation at the ocean and take the family. You cherish everything in the world.

83

You'd never strip the land of trees. You'd plant them. If you have a dog or cat, it probably has a "people name." You work best at any job when you have a stable and predictable home life. You're loyal to those around you.

The M Colors:

Alabaster   Gray
Beige   Turquoise
Blue   Violet
Cream

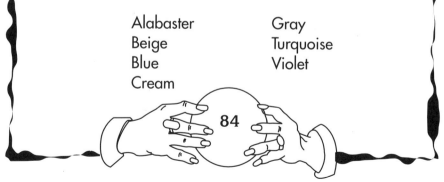

84

The **M** Love Compatibility Guide:

Your main interests are family, family and family, so you might marry early.

<u>Sure Things:</u>	B H K M O
<u>Possibilities:</u>	D I L P S T Y Z
<u>Avoid:</u>	A C E F G J N Q R U V W X

85

Suggested Occupations for the Typical **M**:

Sometimes your own accomplishment is slowed because people drop into your path, and you stop to help them and neglect yourself. You should consider being a counselor or a therapist and get paid for assisting others.

Counselor	Nanny
Doctor	Nurse
Electrician	Parole Officer
Foreman	Sports Medicine Therapist
Investment Advisor	Waitress

86

Organized, Dependable, Loner

"N" should never overdo anything. Moderation or abstinence can be the key words in your life regarding drinking, whatever.

You should never be interfered with when you're completing a laborious project. Others need to stand out of the way and give you your space. Nobody can organize like you, so they shouldn't bother. If people put their fingers into what you're doing, you can get quite upset.

There are times when even you can wear yourself out. You have spurts of being lazy, but that's okay. Give yourself a breather and recover your sagging mental energies.

Because of the way you organize things, you give off a little aura of being flawless. You don't think you are, but you can't help the way others perceive you. People can be jealous, and you might wonder why they don't like you. Put yourself out to get along with others.

Family is important to you even if you don't live with them. They can call you from across the country, sick, and you'll find a way to help them – even if they don't ask. You seem to know when people need help, and you give it. You're one of the few people who can give unconditional love.

You seem to have been born with a lot of information. You can be a loner. You can successfully search for spiritual truth.

The **N** Colors:

Brown

Green

Navy Blue

Sapphire Blue

The **N** Love Compatibility Guide:

Show more of your emotional side, so people can see that you are human. Otherwise, people may never know you to love you.

<u>Sure things:</u>	B H S T Y
<u>Possibilities:</u>	C G I J Q R U X
<u>Avoid:</u>	A D E F K L M N O P V W Z

Suggested Occupations for the Typical **N***:*

You could run a company, work in the medical field or teach religious studies. Should you have piles of paper on your desk, you can locate anything instantly. Your mind is a filing cabinet.

Air Traffic Controller
Certified Public Accountant
CIA or Special Agent

Landscaper
Physician Assistant
Plumber

Intense, Facilitator, Responsible

The **O** Personality:

"O" must learn not take every comment to heart. You really do get your feelings hurt very easily – maybe too easily.

You must talk through problems with people, because you can be too intense. Don't clam up. Tell people gently that you're feeling a little hurt so they can explain what they really mean, which may be different from what you perceive them to mean.

When you set your mind to it, you can resolve family conflicts, because you want peace and compatibility, especially for the sake of your stomach. Otherwise, you'll get sick trying to come up with a solution. You are definitely nurturing.

You can be a perfectionist. Loosen up and don't think that other people agree with you. They don't. Save yourself a lot of hurt, and let them have their own thoughts and ideas.

O loves holidays and weddings and any occasion for the family to get together. You are ingenious, idealistic and innovative. When you're hurt you don't forgive easily, if at all.

96

The ⚪ colors:

Alabaster
Beige
Blue
Cream

Gray
Turquoise
Violet

97

The O Love Compatibility Guide:

O must have a partner in life, but you will need to take a class in charm and negotiating to keep your mate, for you can be very stubborn.

Sure Things: H K M O S T Z
Possibilities: B D I L P Y
Avoid: A C E F G J N Q R U V W X

Suggested Occupations for the Typical O:

You make a terrific agent in almost any arena: entertainment, travel, real estate. You get things accomplished for other people quite easily. You are the facilitator. You are responsible. As for yourself, you need a coach to do for you what you easily do for others.

Home Economics Teacher   Occupational Therapist
Negotiator   Optometrist
Nutritionist   Theatrical Agent

99

Humanitarian, Idealistic, Smart

The **P** Personality:

"P" could have a variety of positions because you must have a challenge mentally. You want to experience everything.

At some point you must stop and make commitments. That word scares you because you like being free to do what you want, when you want. That makes life difficult for others because it's hard to count on your being around tomorrow.

Let your partner handle the checkbook. You've always acted grown up, but that doesn't mean that you're responsible.

101

Life can be difficult for a **P** because you fight your own flights of freedom. You can't envision others not being able to get along with you. All you want is harmony, you think.

Should you have lots of money, you make a great humanitarian. You can fight any cause: for instance, the cause for cancer. You could raise money for it, but you might not know what to do with the person who has it.

P's are idealistic. You don't always see the obvious.

You need to be sure that you've prepared yourself with a fine education so you can use all the talents you have to express. You have a fine mind. You are affable, but **P**'s should try to get a handle on how the real world works.

The **P** Colors:

Light Green	Royal Blue
Pink	White

The **P** *Love Compatibility Guide:*

Multiple marriages would not at all be uncommon for you, if you can even settle down to get married. Finding that right person for you could be impossible because you conceal things. On the other hand, you may not marry at all.

Sure Things: A C E F J L P Q W X
Possibilities: B D G H M O R V
Avoid: I K N S T U Y Z

104

Suggested Occupations for the Typical **P**:

You are magnificent in groups. You love giving your opinions. You could be an actor, speaker, therapist, philosopher, writer or humanitarian. However, leave one on one relating to others.

Accountant
Coach
Editor
Executive Director of
 Non-Profit Agency

Minister
Philosophy Teacher
Pilot
Professional Speaker

Enthusiastic, Creative, Intuitive

The **Q** Personality:

"Q" can be the child of the universe. You're enthusiastic, creative and have loads of drive, but you want everything, and you want it quickly.

That's the reason you might have many different projects all going at the same time. So you won't get bored, you try to handle multiple assignments. You'll get them all done, but you scatter yourself. Sometimes you even get yourself mixed up and confuse others as well. Don't take on too much. Do one or two things well.

107

No doubt you can be successful. You won't tolerate failure for long, but you need to focus and pace yourself. Don't put the cart before the horse to make everything happen at once.

You'll take advantage of every opportunity which comes along. It can appear as if you're conniving. It's not out of malice. You're just want to make it in the world. Watch not to use people.

You're a strange dichotomy. On one hand if you're successful, you can be very philanthropical by contributing to charitable causes. On the other hand, you might be quite penurious when those close to you really need your generosity.

Catastrophes can happen to you, but you seem to come through the fray without much damage.

The Q Colors:

All shades of Blue
Purple

Turquoise

109

The Q Love Compatibility Guide:

Q makes friends very quickly, but relationships may not be long-lasting because you're off networking and forming new ones. You rarely stop to smell the roses. Once you have a family, you can be responsible.

<u>Sure Things:</u>	A C E J L P Q U V X
<u>Possibilities:</u>	F G N R W
<u>Avoid:</u>	B D H I K M O S T Y Z

110

Suggested Occupations for the Typical **Q**:

You have a lot of intuition. You should use it more often. You're witty, bright, can be a team player or the troop commander.

Actor	Fundraiser
Bank President	Grant Writer
College Department Head	Stage Designer
Construction	Travel Agent
Electronics	

111

Persistent, Logical, Distant

The R Personality:

"R" can appear to be cold, uninvolved, distant and caring only for yourself. You almost seem to be detached from other people.

An **R** has a lot of challenges in life which you conquer. Nobody and nothing can keep you down. Listening is not your best attribute. If your parents warned you, "Don't put your finger in the fire!" when you were a child, you did it anyway, because nobody can tell you what to do.

You have to experience everything for yourself. But when you get into trouble because of your actions, you don't complain. You admit to your error, go on and continue down your own path, still not listening to anyone. **R** does what you want to do in your own way.

R's greatest talent is logic. You can think something through and set the action into motion accomplishing what you set out to do. Part of what you do stems from the love of money. You will stay the course if there's money at the end of the rainbow. That's why you may put up with an undesirable situation that others abandon.

You can have accidents because your mind races ahead of your body. Slow down. Life is full of change.

The **R** *Colors:*

Beige   Red
Gold   Yellow
Navy Blue   White
Purple

The **R** Love Compatibility Guide:

You certainly would not want to involve yourself with an emotionally needy partner. Your partner would suffer. Multiple marriages for you are not uncommon. Sometimes it seems as if you don't put yourself out for anyone or anybody.

<u>Sure Things:</u>   A I R U Y

<u>Possibilities:</u>   C D E J L N P Q S V

<u>Avoid:</u>   B F G H K M O T W X Z

Suggested Occupations for the Typical **R**:

You can be brutally persistent in whatever goals you set. Nothing deters you from your goal, not even love. You can be a good idea-person for a company, assigning all the details to others to complete and then bring back to you to assemble.

Adjuster
Collector
Computer Programmer
Electrical Engineer
Farmer

Investigator
Manager
Psychologist
Zoologist

Responsible, Innovative, Ambitious

The **S** Personality:

"S" loves achievement and applause once a goal has been met. Losing isn't a word in your vocabulary.

Even though you can stand alone, whatever you do, you are innovative. **S** wants to stand out. You can be an actor. You can also own a company or run one for someone else because you want to be in charge. Don't be bossy. Ask people politely to do something, and they'll cooperate. Though you can originate change, you don't like it, for it causes internal chaos.

Whenever you hear your still-small voice saying, "Don't do that," or if your muscles tense, pay attention. Intuition is directing you to back off from a person or a situation at that time.

You have a tendency to spend money but can cut back when necessary. If a month ago you made up your mind based on all the information you had, but today you get new information which requires you to change your opinion, you will.

You're flexible even in business. **S** will do what's necessary to get to your goal, but you want to get there in a hurry.

121

You're ambitious, witty, captivating and overachieving. You're ethical. You also have a soft spot for those who are not as lucky as you. You feel that there's a guardian angel on your shoulder.

The **S** Colors:

Black

Emerald Green

Gray

Navy Blue

Wine

122

The **S** Love Compatibility Guide:

S needs to network and meet people whenever you need something because you can be at the right place at the right time, with the right people wanting to be with you.

Sure things: B D G I N O T Z
Possibilities: H K M R S Y
Avoid: A C E F J L P Q U V W X

123

Suggested Occupations for the Typical S:

You're capable of handling stress and obligations because you were probably given chores when you were small. That was practice for the responsible leadership you are capable of exercising as an adult.

Doctor   Nurse
Entrepreneur   Sales
Manager   School Administrator
Marketing and Sales   Teacher
  Consultant   Training Specialist

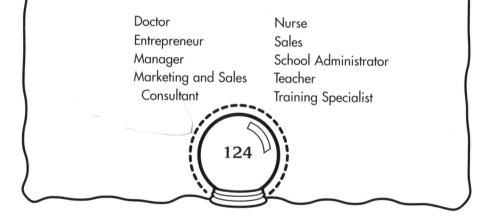

124

Vulnerable, Compassionate, Dedicated

The **T** Personality:

"T" can be taken advantage of easily by lovers who might try to convince you to neglect tradition and have children before marriage. Don't. Partners disappear. Stop living in a fantasy world! You can attract the wrong lovers and friends.

You really do need people emotionally, but watch the friends you keep; no negative people. They can lead you down the wrong path, and you can't turn yourself around without professional help. The danger is that people may try to take advantage of you, and you're such a good person that you won't see ulterior motives. You're vulnerable.

When someone really hurts you to the core, the friendship is over. You might even want to exact revenge. You have a hard time coping with losses – a ring, a job, not counting the loss of a pet or a person. You go through pain of misfortune longer than most people. Consider grief counseling. Whenever a **T** is depressed, you can listen to music or write songs.

T has to work hard for money, so don't give it away to ingrates. You have compassion for everyone in the universe, but people take advantage of your good heart. So keep your head out of the clouds, and think how far you'll go before you help people at your own cost.

Your system does not metabolize alcohol or drugs well. Avoid both unless you want to become addicted.

The T Colors:

Alabaster	Purple
Blue-Green	Violet
Gray	

The **T** Love Compatibility Guide:

Get guidance on how to find the right mate. And should your family dislike a potential life partner, forget marrying that person. It won't work.

<u>Sure Things:</u> G K N O S Y
<u>Possibilities:</u> H M T V W Z
<u>Avoid:</u> A B C D E F I J L P Q R U X

129

Suggested Occupations for the Typical **T**:

You could make an excellent musician. You'd also work well in a nursing home or with children who are having problems. Whatever you do, you are dedicated.

Account Executive	Musician
Buyer	Painter
Composer	Pharmacist
Hotel Manager	Purchaser
Mechanic	Recreational Director

Survivor, Creative, Spiritual

The U Personality:

"U" is a survivor no matter what. You'll make sure that you and your family have food and shelter. Sometimes you appear to be vulnerable, but you aren't. Nobody can take advantage of you.

You can gain a fortune, lose it and regain it. Because your life is never on an even keel, you learned early on how to be miserly. Luck is up and down with you, so you have a tendency to hoard money because you never know when life is going to turn on you again. You are one of a kind and quite novel in your approach to life.

132

You can make friends quickly, but you don't keep them. Energies get scattered. **U** is always in the creating relationships and eager-to-meet-new-people mode.

People look up and wonder why they haven't heard from you for such a long time if you wander back onto their path.

You know how to be charitable when you're not caught up in your own problems. But when you do give, sometimes you want too much in return.

133

The world really isn't against you. Stop fighting and show your loving, spiritual nature and strive for a balance. You can help others without people taking advantage of you and your wallet. You can talk the talk and walk the walk with your talent.

The **U** *Colors:*

All shades of Blue   Turquoise
Purple

134

The **U** Love Compatibility Guide:

U has a lot of hidden feelings, but from outside appearances, others may think that you're heartless. It's also hard for you to relate on an emotional level because your parents skipped giving those lessons to you as a child.

<u>Sure Things:</u>   A C E L Q R V X
<u>Possibilities:</u>   F G J N U W
<u>Avoid:</u>   B D H I K M O P S T Y Z

135

Suggested Occupations for the Typical **U**:

You are also very capable and flexible in career choices. Somewhat a butterfly, **U** excitedly tends to start something new, toss it off to someone else, and begin another venture.

Animal Attendant	Receptionist
Astronomer	Salesperson
Flight Attendant	Therapist
Hostess	Tutor
Preacher	Underwriter

Loyal, Logical, Stubborn

The **V** Personality:

"V" is very loyal. You make the best of friends. If you say you'll do something, you do it. However, at times your interpersonal skills are not the best, for you definitely speak what's on your mind and in no uncertain terms. You'll say, "Why are you running the faucet so long? I resent that you're wasting my water in the universe, too!"

You are cause oriented. It's not uncommon to find you fighting several causes at the same time.

Speaking is no problem. Truly listening is another matter. And even though **V** is logical, it is very difficult to sway you to another's opinion.

At times you feel that you know it all, and no one is as smart as you. You might give the impression that you rule by intimidation because you say something so forcefully that people think that perhaps they are supposed to believe that your words are gospel. Truth is important to you.

V Stubborn? Yes! But you try to avoid arguments because you get nervous quickly.

You demand a lot, but you can give an inordinate amount. You must feel free. You can be your own boss and probably should be.

And once you become successful, few can tell you anything. You can be a long time in your zenith.

You can be religious.

The **V** Colors:

Deep Blue	Violet
Green	White
Turquoise	Yellow

The **V** *Love Compatibility Guide:*

V must learn to negotiate. Otherwise you easily can run off a good partner just at a time when you need one the most. Give your mind a rest.

<u>Sure Things:</u>	E H Q U V X
<u>Possibilities:</u>	A C J P R T Z
<u>Avoid:</u>	B D F G I K L M N O S W Y

Suggested Occupations for the Typical **V**:

You could be a jeweler, a writer or a CPA because you're very good at nitty-gritty details. You're so very logical that sometimes you appear void of emotions until later in life.

Designer	Loan Officer
Drywall and Lathers	Machinist
Engineer	Merchant
Entrepreneur	Project Manager
Jeweler	Physician

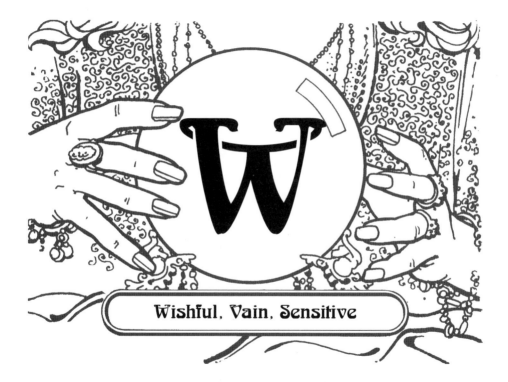

Wishful, Vain, Sensitive

The **W** Personality:

"W" reads people accurately. If you tell someone not to trust another person or a situation, others should listen to you. You're right.

You are a child. The way you were emotionally at six years old is probably how you will be at age one hundred. If you were insulted three years ago, you will remember what a person said

144

and maybe what the person was wearing when he said it. No escaping your "video tape memory."

Once you've formed an opinion, only God could change it. Perhaps.

Your vanity can be your downfall. You are willful and want your own way, and will do about anything to get it. Nothing must stand in your way.

145

You'll help people if you don't have to go out of your way because you want your environment to stay on an even keel. You don't like change one bit. People have to watch what they say to you and how they say it because your feelings get hurt far too easily.

All of your life you need a lot of encouragement. And, like a child, if you're scolded, you pout until someone apologizes. And it won't be you.

You love kicking your heels up with friends.

The **W** Colors:

Emerald Green   Royal Blue
Gold   Wine
Orange   Yellow
Red

147

The **W** Love Compatibility Guide:

W can play and get into trouble with the opposite sex, but you want your partner to keep the home fires burning until you get home.

<u>Sure thing:</u>	E L P X
<u>Possibilities:</u>	A C Q T U Z
<u>Avoid:</u>	B D F G H I J K M N O R S V W Y

148

Suggested Occupations for the Typical **W**:

Once you see the big picture on a job, you go for it. You'd make a great general in the Armed Forces, enjoying everyone clicking heels, saluting and doing your bidding. The problem could arise on your way up in the ranks trying to get you to obey orders. You need to take an occupational choice test to uncover your true skills.

Artist
Costume Designer
Department Manager
Human Resources Manager

Military Comander
Minister
Scientist
Teacher

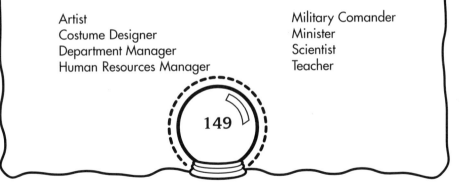

149

Dramatic, Responsible, Positive

The **X** Personality:

"X" definitely has a sense of the dramatic – maybe even of the Greek tragedy. With your theatrical flair, it's hard not to notice you.

You are an original, and your outlook is one of a kind, always trying to find a better method. You are prone to do everything in excess.

When you work, you work too hard; and when you play, the same. You also love too hard. Whatever you're given to do, you do it well and with passion.

151

X will never force an outlook upon others. You will not take the leadership role unless you feel that nobody else can do it as well as you. You assess the situation first, then jump in if necessary. You're responsible. Failure is not acceptable.

You need to have a lot to do and must be surrounded with love and people and even pets. You are not a fly-by-night.

X's positive attitude is contagious – especially when you fight causes. Others will rally around you when you take on the unfortunate.

152

You're grateful. You help others, and others come to your rescue. Like an injured lion with a thorn in it's paw, you can lick a wound longer than most.

The **X** Colors:

Beige　　　　　　　　　Purple
Navy Blue　　　　　　Yellow

The **X** *Love Compatibility Guide:*

When you give your loyalty, it's forever; but you won't give it until you know that the person is worthy and will also return what you freely give.

Sure things: F J L P Q U V W
Possibilities: C H N X
Avoid: A B D E G I K M O R S T Y Z

Suggested Occupations for the Typical **X**:

You could be a trapeze artist, a dare devil on the wings of a biplane, work underwater on a science project or be in space to interview an astronaut for a news article. You can be an explorer, since you love discovering new lands. And perhaps only you could do all of these at the same time. But you do have to watch that you complete what you begin.

Comedian
Explorer
Geologist
Inventor

Navigator
Photographer
Preacher
Zoo Keeper

155

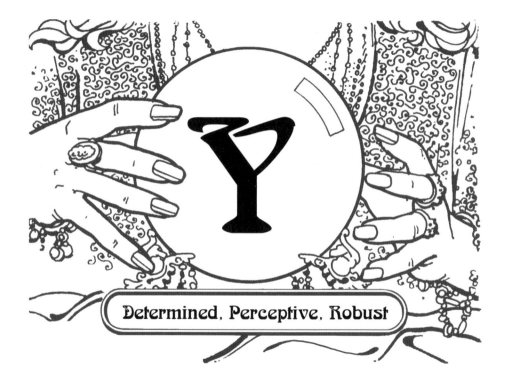

Determined, Perceptive, Robust

The **Y** Personality:

"Y" can put every business and house in order. Just give you the opportunity and you'll stay with it until it's finished. You don't need to be prodded to do your work, because whatever you take on becomes play for you.

"Time is of the essence" is something written just for you. Every minute of every hour of every day you employ it to its fullest. No one would find you at the water cooler.

Some people think you don't stop to smell the roses, but you do, after you've accomplished what you set out to do.

Y can determine your own success because you'll stay on your path until you get what you want. Instant gratification is not in your vocabulary.

You'll postpone your desires to accomplish the task at hand. Because your early life can be full of responsibilities, your dreams may not come true until later, when you start living life. Watch how many obligations you assume. They can pile up on you to the point of being unbearable. You'll handle them, but at what price?

Y can push their children too hard to take advantage of the opportunities you might not have had earlier on in life. You're too idealistic. You think everything is going to turn out right. It doesn't always.

The **Y** *Colors:*

Black

Emerald Green

Gray

Navy Blue

Wine

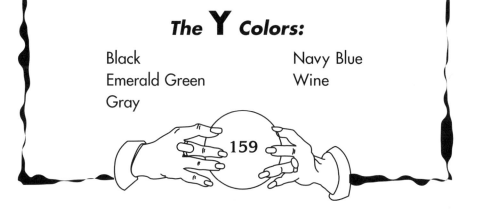

The **Y** Love Compatibility Guide:

Because your success can come later in life, sharing your success is easy. You love for others to have some of what you have, and that makes you an easy target. Be sure to bank some of your money.

<u>Sure Things:</u>   B G N R T Z
<u>Possibilities:</u>   D I K M O Q S U V W X Y
<u>Avoid:</u>   A C E F H J L P

160

Suggested Occupations for the Typical **Y**:

You're determined, perceptive and robust. If you follow your instincts, success more readily happens. It's a gift. Listen to your feelings. You're being protected.

Administrator	Computer Operator
Advertising Manager	Mechanic
Budget Analyst	Stock Broker

161

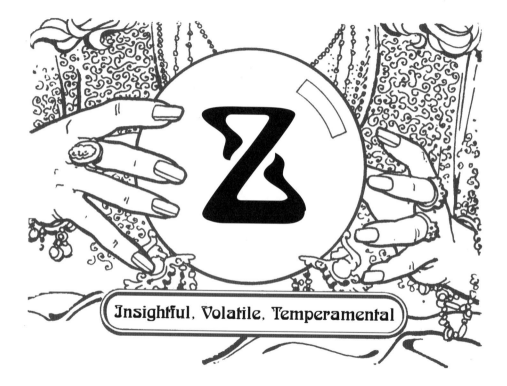

Insightful, Volatile, Temperamental

The **Z** Personality:

"Z" can have some unexplainable insights, but you might not understand them yourself. Just accept them as brilliance and follow up on your hunches.

You cannot be crossed in any manner because, if you are, you will bellow. And since your memory is long, you'll hold a grudge against anyone who disappointed you. Bouncing back is a great talent that you have. It's a good thing, because your life can be full of swings from one end of the spectrum to the other. You seem to get used to it at an early age.

You could buy a sob story and get taken advantage of in the process. If that happens, try not to be too hard on yourself when you make the wrong decision. Don't dwell on how it happened or who caused it to happen. Just know that you made the best judgment you could at the time and let it go. Get on with looking for recognition in another area. Recognition is a magic word for a **Z**.

You'll go out of your way to help anyone who gives you the appreciation you know you deserve. **Z** should never work around dynamite. You're far too volatile. The whole place could blow once your temper explodes. You're a magnet. You attract people.

Money is important to you. You need it for the various projects you juggle and for the home and family you adore, but don't take financial chances.

The Z Colors:

Alabaster   Purple
Blue-Green   Violet
Gray

The **Z** *Love Compatibility Guide:*

People don't easily forget you. They either love you or hate you.

<u>Sure Things:</u>   A G K O S Y

<u>Possibilities:</u>   B D M T V W Z

<u>Avoid:</u>   C E F H I J L N P Q R U X

Suggested Occupations for the Typical **Z**:

Whatever you decide to do, you could make a name for yourself. You know that you're talented, but it's an ego booster when you're applauded.

Dental Assistant
Human Resource Director
Marketing Research
Postal Clerk

Psychic
Running a Homeless Shelter
Underwriter

Other Titles By Great Quotations

201 Best Things Ever Said
The ABC's of Parenting
As a Cat Thinketh
The Best of Friends
The Birthday Astrologer
Chicken Soup & Other Yiddish Say
Cornerstones of Success
Don't Deliberate ... Litigate!
Fantastic Father, Dependable Dad
Global Wisdom
Golden Years, Golden Words
Grandma, I Love You
Growing up in Toyland
Happiness is Found Along The Way
Hollywords
Hooked on Golf
In Celebration of Women
Inspirations Compelling Food for Thought
I'm Not Over the Hill
Let's Talk Decorating
Life's Lessons
Life's Simple Pleasures
A Light Heart Lives Long
Money for Nothing, Tips for Free

Mother, I Love You
Motivating Quotes for Motivated People
Mrs. Aesop's Fables
Mrs. Murphy's Laws
Mrs. Webster's Dictionary
My Daughter, My Special Friend
Other Species
Parenting 101
Reflections
Romantic Rhapsody
The Secret Language of Men
The Secret Language of Women
Some Things Never Change
The Sports Page
Sports Widow
Stress or Sanity
Teacher is Better than Two Books
Teenage of Insanity
Thanks from the Heart
Things You'll Learn if You Live Long Enough
Wedding Wonders
Working Women's World
Interior Design for Idiots
Dear Mr. President

GREAT QUOTATIONS PUBLISHING COMPANY
1967 Quincy Court
Glendale Heights, IL 60139 - 2045
Phone (630) 582-2800
Fax (630) 582- 2813